How To Make Money on Facebook

By

Dr Chris Egbu

Author

Of

- How to Make Money Online

- How to Gain Clients

- How to Make Money with a Chatbot

- 20 Easy Steps to Be More Productive,

- Entrepreneurial Finance-How To Raise Capital to Start Your Business

&

- Newways of Employee Empowerment

Also available on Amazon

How To Make Money on Facebook

Copyright © 2024 by Chris Egbu

Cover design by Samuel Effiong

Cover copyright © 2024 by Centre for Public Service Productivity& Development.

Table of Contents

Table of Contents

Table of Contents

How To Make Money on Facebook

Introduction

A. The power of Facebook as a business platform

B. Overview of the book's purpose and structure

A. The Power of Facebook as a Business Platform

In today's digital age, social media platforms have revolutionized the way businesses connect with their audience, and Facebook stands out as a powerful player in this realm. With over 2.8 billion monthly active users, Facebook offers an unparalleled opportunity to reach a vast audience and tap into a thriving online community. From small startups to multinational corporations, businesses of all sizes can leverage the immense potential of Facebook to grow their brand, engage with customers, and ultimately make money.

Facebook's extensive reach, advanced targeting capabilities, and diverse range of advertising options make it a valuable platform for businesses across industries. Whether you're looking to sell products, offer services, or monetize your content, Facebook provides a fertile ground for you to achieve your financial goals and establish a successful online presence.

B. Overview of the Book's Purpose and Structure

The purpose of this book is to guide you through the process of making money on Facebook, providing you with practical strategies, insights, and tips to maximize your success on this dynamic platform. We will delve into various aspects of Facebook as a business platform, from setting up a strong foundation to monetizing your presence and scaling your business.

The book is structured comprehensively and logically, taking you through the essential steps required to effectively monetize Facebook. Each chapter focuses on a specific topic, providing in-depth explanations, real-world examples, and actionable advice. Whether you're a beginner looking to establish your online presence or an experienced marketer seeking to optimize your Facebook strategy, this book will offer valuable insights and guidance to help you achieve your financial objectives.

By the end of this book, you will have a solid understanding of how to effectively leverage Facebook's features, tools, and advertising options to generate revenue, build a loyal customer base, and create a thriving online business. It's time to harness the power of Facebook and unlock the lucrative opportunities that await you in the world of social media monetization.

Chapter 1. Understanding the Facebook Landscape

A. History and growth of Facebook

B. Facebook's user demographics and reach

C. Overview of Facebook's advertising and monetization options

A. History and Growth of Facebook

To fully grasp the potential of Facebook as a business platform, it's important to understand its history and remarkable growth. Facebook was founded by Mark Zuckerberg and his college roommates in 2004 as a social networking platform for Harvard University students. It quickly expanded to other universities and eventually opened its doors to the general public in 2006. Since then, Facebook has experienced exponential growth, becoming the largest social media platform in the world.

B. Facebook's User Demographics and Reach

Facebook boasts an extensive user base, making it a valuable platform for businesses to connect with a wide range of individuals. The platform's user demographics are diverse, spanning different age groups, geographical locations, and interests. While originally popular among college students,

Facebook's user base now includes people of all ages, from teenagers to senior citizens.

With over 2.8 billion monthly active users as of 2021, Facebook offers unprecedented reach. This global presence allows businesses to target specific audiences based on demographics, interests, behaviours, and more, ensuring that their content and advertisements reach the right people at the right time.

C. Overview of Facebook's Advertising and Monetization Options

Facebook provides businesses with a multitude of advertising and monetization options to generate revenue and achieve their financial objectives. Some key options include:

Facebook Ads: The platform's robust advertising system allows businesses to create targeted ads that appear in users' News Feeds, Instagram feeds, Messenger, and other placements. Facebook Ads Manager provides sophisticated targeting capabilities, budget control, and performance tracking to optimize ad campaigns.

Pages and Business Manager: Facebook Pages offer businesses a dedicated space to showcase their brand, products, and services. Business Manager provides tools for managing multiple Pages, ad accounts, and permissions, enabling efficient campaign management.

Sponsored Content and Influencer Marketing: Businesses can collaborate with influencers or content creators to promote their products or services. Sponsored content can take the form of posts, videos, or stories, reaching the influencer's engaged audience.

Facebook Marketplace: This feature allows businesses to sell products directly to Facebook users within their local communities. It provides a convenient and accessible platform for e-commerce transactions.

Audience Network: Facebook's Audience Network extends advertising reach beyond the Facebook platform, allowing businesses to monetize their apps and websites by displaying Facebook ads to their users.

Understanding these advertising and monetization options is crucial for businesses looking to leverage Facebook's immense potential to generate revenue and maximize their online presence.

By familiarizing yourself with the history, demographics, and advertising opportunities that Facebook offers, you will be well-equipped to navigate the platform and make informed decisions on how to effectively monetize your presence on this thriving social media giant.

Chapter 2. Building a Strong Foundation

A. Setting up a Facebook Business Page

B. Optimizing your profile and branding

C. Understanding Facebook's algorithm and optimizing reach

A. Setting up a Facebook Business Page

Setting up a Facebook Business Page is the first step towards establishing a strong foundation for your presence on the platform. Follow these key steps:

Create a Page: Visit the Facebook Business Page creation page and select the appropriate category for your business. Provide essential details such as your business name, category, and contact information.

Add Profile and Cover Photos: Choose visually appealing and representative images for your profile and cover photos. These images should align with your brand identity and capture users' attention.

Complete Your About Section: Craft a compelling and informative description of your business in the "About" section. Include relevant keywords to enhance discoverability.

Customize Your Page Tabs: Tailor your Page's tabs to highlight the most important information and features for your audience. Consider including tabs for services, products, reviews, or events, depending on your business type.

B. Optimizing Your Profile and Branding

To make the most of your Facebook Business Page and create a strong brand presence, consider the following:

Consistent Branding: Maintain consistent branding elements, such as your logo, colour scheme, and brand voice, across your Page. This helps users recognize and associate your brand with your content.

Compelling Content Strategy: Develop a content strategy that aligns with your target audience's interests and needs. Plan a mix of engaging posts, including informative articles, visually appealing images, videos, and interactive content.

Engage with Your Audience: Actively engage with your audience by responding to comments, messages, and reviews. Encourage conversation and build relationships with your followers.

Utilize Facebook's Features: Take advantage of features like Facebook Live, Stories, and Events to connect with your audience in real time and create interactive experiences.

C. Understanding Facebook's Algorithm and Optimizing Reach

Facebook's algorithm determines which posts appear in users' News Feeds, making it essential to understand and optimize for maximum reach. Consider the following strategies:

Quality Content: Publish high-quality, relevant, and engaging content that resonates with your audience. The algorithm prioritizes posts that generate meaningful interactions.

Timing and Frequency: Experiment with different posting times and frequencies to identify when your audience is most active. Consistency is key, but avoid overwhelming your followers with excessive posts.

Encourage Engagement: Prompt your audience to like, comment, and share your posts. Ask questions, run polls, or use interactive elements to encourage participation.

Utilize Facebook Insights: Regularly review Facebook Insights to gain valuable data about your audience's behaviour, engagement metrics, and post-performance. Use this data to refine your content strategy and optimize reach.

By focusing on setting up a compelling Facebook Business Page, optimizing your profile and branding, and understanding and leveraging Facebook's algorithm, you can establish a strong foundation that maximizes your reach and engagement on the platform. This will set the stage for effectively monetizing your Facebook presence in the subsequent chapters.

Chapter 3. Creating Engaging Content

A. Identifying your target audience

B. Crafting compelling posts and visuals

C. Strategies for increasing engagement and building a loyal following

A. Identifying Your Target Audience

To create engaging content on Facebook, it's crucial to have a deep understanding of your target audience. Consider the following steps:

Demographic Research: Identify key demographic information about your audience, such as age, gender, location, and language. This will help you tailor your content to their preferences.

Psychographic Analysis: Dive deeper into your audience's interests, values, motivations, and behaviours. Understand their pain points, aspirations, and what resonates with them emotionally.

Audience Segmentation: Divide your audience into segments based on shared characteristics. This allows you to create more personalized and targeted content for each group.

B. Crafting Compelling Posts and Visuals

Once you have a clear understanding of your target audience, you can create content that captures their attention and drives engagement. Consider the following strategies:

Storytelling: Use storytelling to evoke emotions and connect with your audience on a deeper level. Craft narratives that are relatable, inspiring, or entertaining.

Visual Appeal: Include high-quality images, videos, and graphics in your posts to make them visually appealing and eye-catching. Use professional design tools or leverage Facebook's native editing features.

Varied Content Formats: Experiment with different content formats, such as text-based posts, images, videos, infographics, or live videos. This keeps your content fresh and caters to different preferences.

Calls to Action: Encourage your audience to take action by including clear and compelling calls to action (CTAs) in your posts. Examples include "Like this post," "Share your thoughts in the comments," or "Visit our website for more information."

C. Strategies for Increasing Engagement and Building a Loyal Following

Engagement and building a loyal following are essential for long-term success on Facebook. Implement the following strategies to boost engagement and foster a loyal community:

Respond to Comments and Messages: Promptly reply to comments, messages, and inquiries from your audience. Show genuine interest, address concerns, and foster conversations.

Encourage User-Generated Content (UGC): Encourage your audience to share their experiences, stories, or creations related to your brand. UGC not only boosts engagement but also builds a sense of community.

Run Contests and Giveaways: Organize contests, sweepstakes, or giveaways to incentivize engagement and reward your audience. This can include liking, commenting, sharing, or creating user-generated content.

Collaborate with Influencers or Partners: Partner with influencers or complementary brands to expand your reach and tap into their engaged audience. Collaborative content and cross-promotion can drive engagement and attract new followers.

Consistency and Frequency: Maintain a consistent posting schedule to stay on top of your audience's minds. Regularly provide fresh and valuable content to keep them engaged and coming back for more.

Remember, building a loyal following takes time and effort. Focus on nurturing relationships, providing value, and creating a positive community experience to foster long-term engagement and brand advocacy.

By identifying your target audience, crafting compelling content and visuals, and implementing strategies to increase engagement and build a loyal following, you can create an engaging Facebook presence that resonates with your audience and drives meaningful interactions.

Chapter 4. Leveraging Facebook Advertising

A. Introduction to Facebook Ads Manager

B. Targeting options and audience segmentation

C. Creating effective ad campaigns and optimizing performance

A. Introduction to Facebook Ads Manager

Facebook Ads Manager is a powerful tool that allows businesses to create, manage, and optimize their ad campaigns on the platform. It provides a wide range of features and functionalities to help you reach your target audience effectively. Here's an overview of Facebook Ads Manager:

Ad Campaign Structure: Facebook Ads Manager organizes your campaigns into three levels: Campaign, Ad Set, and Ad. A campaign represents your advertising objective, while the ad set defines your targeting, budget, and schedule. The ad level includes the actual creative elements of your ads.

Ad Formats: Facebook offers various ad formats, including image ads, video ads, carousel ads, collection ads, and more. Each format has unique features and allows you to showcase your products, services, or content in different ways.

Ad Placement: Facebook offers multiple ad placement options, such as News Feed, Instagram feeds, Stories, Messenger, and Audience Network. You can select specific placements based on where your target audience is most likely to engage with your content.

B. Targeting Options and Audience Segmentation

Facebook provides robust targeting options to help you reach your desired audience. By segmenting your audience effectively, you can create highly targeted ads that resonate with specific groups. Consider the following targeting options:

Demographics: Target users based on age, gender, location, language, education level, and more. This allows you to narrow down your audience and reach those who are most likely to be interested in your offerings.

Interests and Behaviors: Define your audience based on their interests, hobbies, activities, and behaviours. This helps you target individuals who have demonstrated specific preferences or engaged with related content.

Custom Audiences: Utilize Custom Audiences to target users who have already interacted with your business. This can include website visitors, app users, or existing customer lists. Custom Audiences allow for retargeting and personalized messaging.

Lookalike Audiences: Create Lookalike Audiences to reach new users who share similar characteristics to your existing customers or Custom Audiences. Facebook analyzes data and finds users who are likely to be interested in your business.

C. Creating Effective Ad Campaigns and Optimizing Performance

To create effective ad campaigns on Facebook, follow these strategies to optimize your performance:

Compelling Ad Copy: Craft persuasive and concise ad copy that grabs attention and communicates the value proposition of your product or service. Highlight benefits, use strong calls to action, and test different messaging approaches.

Eye-Catching Visuals: Use high-quality images or videos that capture attention and align with your brand identity. Ensure your visuals are visually engaging, relevant to your target audience, and comply with Facebook's ad guidelines.

A/B Testing: Experiment with different ad variations, such as different headlines, images, or calls to action, to identify the most effective combinations. A/B testing helps you optimize your ads based on real data and improve performance.

Ad Optimization: Monitor your ad campaigns regularly and track key metrics such as click-through rates (CTR), conversions, and return on ad spend (ROAS). Use Facebook Ads Manager's optimization features to automatically allocate the budget to the best-performing ads or ad sets.

Retargeting and Funnel Optimization: Implement retargeting strategies to reach users who have shown interest in your business but haven't converted. Create custom audiences based on user behaviour and design tailored ads to move them further down the conversion funnel.

Ongoing Analysis and Iteration: Continuously analyze your ad performance, audience insights, and feedback to refine and improve your campaigns. Adjust targeting, creative elements, and bidding strategies based on real-time data to maximize your results.

By leveraging Facebook Ads Manager, utilizing targeting options effectively, and implementing strategies for creating compelling ad campaigns and optimizing performance, you can harness the full potential of Facebook advertising and achieve your business objectives.

Chapter 5. Monetizing Your Facebook Presence

A. Developing a monetization strategy

B. Exploring revenue streams such as sponsored content, partnerships, and affiliate marketing

C. Selling products or services directly through Facebook

A. Developing a Monetization Strategy

To monetize your Facebook presence effectively, it's important to develop a well-defined strategy. Consider the following steps:

Define Your Goals: Determine the specific goals you want to achieve through monetization. This could include generating passive income, driving sales for your products or services, or increasing brand awareness.

Understand Your Audience: Gain a deep understanding of your audience's needs, preferences, and pain points. This will help you tailor your monetization strategy to provide value and resonate with your followers.

Choose the Right Approach: Evaluate the different monetization approaches available and select the ones that align with your goals and audience. This could include sponsored content, partnerships, affiliate marketing, or selling products directly.

Balance Quality and Monetization: Strive to maintain a balance between monetization and providing valuable content. Ensure that your monetization efforts are transparent, authentic, and enhance the overall user experience.

B. Exploring Revenue Streams such as Sponsored Content, Partnerships, and Affiliate Marketing

Sponsored Content: Collaborate with brands and create sponsored content that aligns with your audience's interests. Ensure that the sponsored content is relevant, valuable, and fits organically within your content strategy. Disclose any sponsored relationships to maintain transparency.

Partnerships: Explore partnerships with complementary brands or influencers in your niche. This can involve cross-promotion, joint content creation, or co-branding initiatives. Partnerships can help you expand your reach and tap into new audiences.

Affiliate Marketing: Join affiliate programs and promote products or services relevant to your audience. Earn a commission for every sale or referral made through your unique affiliate links. Be transparent about your affiliate partnerships to maintain trust.

Branded Content Creator Tools: Utilize Facebook's Branded Content Creator Tools, if available, to streamline partnerships and collaborations. These tools help you disclose sponsored relationships, track performance, and provide valuable insights to your partners.

Furthermore, Facebook's Branded Content Creator Tools are also features and resources designed to help creators, influencers, and publishers collaborate with brands and create sponsored content on the platform. These tools enable seamless partnerships and provide various capabilities to enhance branded content creation and tracking. Here are some key features of Facebook's Branded Content Creator Tools:

1. Branded Content Tag: The Branded Content Tag allows creators to tag the brand or sponsor they are collaborating within their posts. This tag helps provide transparency to the audience that the content is a paid partnership.

2. Rights Manager: This tool enables content owners, such as publishers or influencers, to protect and manage their intellectual property rights. It helps identify and manage instances of unauthorized or infringing content.

3. Brand Collabs Manager: The Brand Collabs Manager is a marketplace where brands can connect with creators for potential collaborations.

It facilitates the discovery of relevant creators based on specific audience demographics, interests, and engagement metrics.

4. Insights and Metrics: Creators can access insights and metrics related to their branded content posts, such as reach, engagement, and audience demographics. These analytics provide valuable information for measuring the success and impact of sponsored content.

5. Content Control and Targeting: Creators have control over the visibility and targeting of their branded content. They can set restrictions on the intended audience, geographic locations, or age groups for their sponsored posts.

6. Collaborative Post Creation: The Branded Content Creator Tools allow for shared post creation between creators and brands. This feature streamlines the collaboration process by enabling both parties to contribute to the content, such as images, captions, or video assets.

7. Advertiser Control: Brands can boost or promote the branded content posts as paid ads to extend their reach and target specific audiences.

It's worth noting that Facebook's Branded Content Creator Tools may evolve as the platform introduces new features and updates. Creators and brands can leverage these tools to create engaging and transparent sponsored content experiences for their audiences.

C. Selling Products or Services Directly through Facebook

Facebook Shop: Set up a Facebook Shop to showcase and sell your products directly on the platform. Customize your shop with product images, descriptions, pricing, and inventory management. Enable features like product tags and collections to enhance the shopping experience.

Facebook Marketplace: List your products or services on Facebook Marketplace, a platform where users can discover, buy, and sell items locally or nationally. Ensure your listings are accurate, visually appealing, and priced competitively.

Messenger for Business: Leverage Messenger for Business to provide personalized customer support, answer inquiries, and guide potential customers through the purchasing process. Utilize automated responses and chatbots to handle common queries efficiently.

Facebook Live Shopping: Utilize the Facebook Live feature to showcase and sell products in real time. Engage with your audience, demonstrate product features, and provide exclusive offers during live sessions. Encourage viewers to make purchases directly through comments or links.

Remember to comply with Facebook's policies and guidelines related to monetization and selling products. Regularly analyze your monetization efforts, track performance metrics, and adapt your strategy based on customer feedback and market trends.

By developing a monetization strategy, exploring revenue streams like sponsored content, partnerships, and affiliate marketing, and leveraging Facebook's e-commerce features, you can effectively monetize your Facebook presence and turn your online presence into a revenue-generating platform.

Chapter 6. Growing and Scaling Your Facebook Business

A. Strategies for increasing your reach and visibility

B. Building a community and fostering customer loyalty

C. Scaling your business through Facebook groups, events, and collaborations

A. Strategies for Increasing Your Reach and Visibility

To grow and scale your Facebook business, it's crucial to increase your reach and visibility. Consider the following strategies:

Consistent and Quality Content: Regularly create and share high-quality content that provides value to your audience. This can include informative posts, engaging visuals, videos, and interactive content. Consistency builds trust and keeps your brand top-of-mind.

Utilize Facebook Ads: Leverage Facebook Ads to reach a wider audience beyond your existing followers. Use targeting options effectively to reach users who are likely to be interested in your products or services. Experiment with different ad formats and optimize your campaigns for better results.

Engage with Relevant Communities: Actively participate in relevant Facebook groups, communities, and forums where your target audience is present. Provide helpful insights, answer questions, and establish yourself as an authority in your niche. Avoid being overly promotional and focus on building genuine connections.

Collaborate with Influencers: Partner with influencers or industry experts who have a significant following and influence in your niche. Collaborative campaigns, such as sponsored posts or co-created content, can help you tap into their audience and expand your reach.

B. Building a Community and Fostering Customer Loyalty

Building a community and fostering customer loyalty are integral to sustainable growth. Consider the following strategies:

Encourage Engagement: Prompt your audience to engage with your content by asking questions, running polls, or requesting user-generated content. Respond to comments and messages promptly, fostering a sense of community and making your followers feel heard.

Provide Value: Continuously provide value to your audience through informative and educational content. Share tips, tutorials, industry insights, or exclusive offers that are relevant to your audience's interests and needs.

Offer Exclusive Benefits: Reward your loyal followers with exclusive benefits, such as early access to new products, discounts, or special promotions. Make them feel appreciated and part of an exclusive community.

User-Generated Content: Encourage your audience to create and share content related to your brand. This can include testimonials, reviews, or creative user-generated content. Repost and showcase user-generated content to foster a sense of belonging and community.

C. Scaling Your Business through Facebook Groups, Events, and Collaborations

Facebook Groups: Create and nurture a Facebook group centred around your brand, industry, or a specific interest related to your business. Encourage discussions, share valuable content, and provide a platform for your community to connect and engage with each other.

Facebook Events: Host virtual or in-person events using Facebook Events. This can include webinars, workshops, product launches, or networking opportunities. Events help you reach a larger audience, generate excitement, and build relationships with your customers.

Collaborations and Cross-Promotion: Collaborate with other businesses or influencers in your industry to cross-promote each other's products or services. This can expand your reach and introduce your brand to new audiences.

Explore Facebook Marketplace: If applicable to your business, consider utilizing Facebook Marketplace to reach a wider audience and sell your products or services directly to interested users.

Regularly analyze your growth strategies, track key metrics, and adapt your approach based on the feedback and preferences of your audience. Remember to stay authentic, prioritize building relationships, and provide value to your community.

By implementing strategies to increase your reach and visibility, building a community, and leveraging Facebook groups, events, and collaborations, you can effectively grow and scale your Facebook business while fostering customer loyalty and engagement.

Chapter 7. Analyzing and Optimizing Results

A. Tracking and analyzing key metrics

B. Identifying areas for improvement and optimization

C. A/B testing and experimenting with different strategies

A. Tracking and Analyzing Key Metrics

To effectively analyze and optimize your Facebook marketing efforts, it's important to track and analyze key metrics. Consider the following steps:

Define Your Key Performance Indicators (KPIs): Identify the metrics that align with your business goals. This could include reach, engagement, click-through rates (CTR), conversion rates, return on ad spend (ROAS), or customer acquisition cost (CAC).

Utilize Facebook Insights: Use Facebook Insights to gain valuable data about your page, audience demographics, post reach, engagement, and more. Insights provide insights into what content performs well and how your audience is responding.

Custom Tracking: Implement custom tracking by using Facebook Pixel or UTM parameters to track specific actions on your website, such as conversions, purchases, or lead generation.

UTM parameters, also known as UTM tags or UTM codes, are short snippets of text added to the end of a URL to track and analyze the performance of marketing campaigns. UTM stands for "Urchin Tracking Module," which was the original name of the analytics software that Google acquired and later developed into Google Analytics.

UTM parameters allow you to measure the effectiveness of your Facebook campaigns in driving desired outcomes.

UTM parameters consist of key-value pairs appended to a URL. When a user clicks on a URL with UTM parameters, the information contained in those parameters is sent to the website's analytics tool, allowing for detailed tracking and analysis of the traffic source.

The five main UTM parameters are:

1. utm_source: This parameter identifies the source of the traffic, such as a search engine, social media platform, or newsletter. For example, utm_source=facebook.

2. utm_medium: This parameter specifies the medium or marketing channel that brought the traffic, such as email, CPC (cost-per-click) advertising, or social media. For example, utm_medium=email.

3. utm_campaign: This parameter is used to track a specific marketing campaign or promotion. It helps differentiate between different initiatives within the same source and medium. For example, utm_campaign=spring_sale.

4. utm_term: This parameter is typically used for paid search campaigns to track the specific keywords or terms that triggered the ad. For example, utm_term=running+shoes.

5. utm_content: This parameter is used to differentiate between different versions or elements of the same campaign. It can be helpful for A/B testing or tracking the performance of different ad placements or variations. For example, utm_content=sidebar+banner.

When combined, these UTM parameters provide detailed insights into the effectiveness of different marketing efforts, allowing marketers to measure the success of specific campaigns, identify the most effective traffic sources, and optimize their marketing strategies based on data-driven insights.

B. Identifying Areas for Improvement and Optimization

Performance Analysis: Regularly review your metrics and identify areas that need improvement. Pay attention to low-performing ads, targeting options, or content types that aren't resonating with your audience.

Audience Insights: Dive deeper into audience insights to understand the characteristics and behaviors of your target audience. Identify patterns and preferences to refine your targeting strategies and create more relevant content.

Ad Creative and Copy: Evaluate the performance of your ad creative and copy. Test different visuals, headlines calls to action, or ad formats to identify what resonates best with your audience. Optimize your creative elements based on data-driven insights.

Landing Page Experience: Assess the performance of your landing pages or website. Ensure they are optimized for conversions, load quickly, and provide a seamless user experience. Make necessary adjustments to improve the conversion rate.

C. A/B Testing and Experimenting with Different Strategies

A/B Testing: Conduct A/B tests by creating variations of your ads, landing pages, or targeting options. Test one variable at a time, such as headlines, visuals, or audience segments, to identify the most effective elements. Measure the performance and implement changes accordingly.

Experiment with Different Strategies: Continuously experiment with different strategies to uncover new opportunities. This can include testing new ad formats, exploring different targeting options, or experimenting with content themes. Keep track of the results and iterate on successful strategies.

Ad Scheduling and Budget Allocation: Experiment with different ad scheduling and budget allocation strategies to optimize your campaigns. Test different days of the week, times of the day, or budget distribution to identify the most cost-effective and impactful approach.

Audience Exclusions: Explore audience exclusions to refine your targeting. Exclude audiences that have already converted or shown no interest in your offerings. This helps you allocate your budget more efficiently and focus on reaching new potential customers.

Regularly review your findings, adapt your strategies based on data-driven insights, and continue testing and optimizing for better results. Keep up with industry trends, stay informed about Facebook's updates, and be open to new strategies and techniques that can enhance your Facebook marketing efforts.

By tracking and analyzing key metrics, identifying areas for improvement, and conducting A/B tests and experiments, you can optimize your Facebook marketing campaigns and achieve better performance and results.

Chapter 8. Beyond Facebook: Integrating with Other Platforms

A. Leveraging Facebook's integration options with other social media platforms

B. Exploring cross-platform marketing and advertising strategies

C. Building an omnichannel presence to maximize your revenue potential

A. Leveraging Facebook's Integration Options with Other Social Media Platforms

Facebook offers integration options that allow you to connect and leverage other social media platforms. Consider the following:

Instagram Integration: Since Facebook owns Instagram, you can easily integrate your Facebook page with an Instagram business account. This allows you to manage both platforms from a single interface, cross-post content, and access additional features like Instagram Shopping.

Messenger Integration: Integrate Facebook Messenger with your website or other customer touchpoints. This enables seamless communication, allowing customers to reach you directly through Messenger and providing personalized support.

Third-Party Integration: Explore third-party tools or platforms that integrate with Facebook, such as social media management tools or customer relationship management (CRM) systems. These integrations can streamline your workflow, automate processes, and enhance your overall marketing efforts.

B. Exploring Cross-Platform Marketing and Advertising Strategies

To maximize your reach and engagement, it's important to implement cross-platform marketing and advertising strategies. Consider the following approaches:

Audience Targeting: Utilize data from Facebook to inform your targeting efforts on other platforms. Leverage Facebook's audience insights to identify the characteristics and interests of your target audience, and apply these insights when advertising on other platforms like Instagram, Twitter, or LinkedIn.

Coordinated Campaigns: Develop coordinated campaigns across multiple platforms, ensuring consistent messaging and branding. Align your content, visuals, and offers to create a seamless customer experience across platforms.

Retargeting: Implement cross-platform retargeting strategies to engage with users who have shown interest in your brand on Facebook. Use tools like Facebook Pixel or third-party retargeting platforms to reach these users on other platforms, such as Google Ads or LinkedIn Ads.

Collaborations with Influencers: Collaborate with influencers who have a presence on multiple platforms. This allows you to tap into their audience across different platforms and benefit from their reach and influence.

C. Building an Omnichannel Presence to Maximize Your Revenue Potential

Building an omnichannel presence involves establishing a cohesive experience across various channels to maximize your revenue potential.

Consider the following steps:

Consistent Branding: Maintain consistent branding elements, such as logos, color schemes, and messaging, across all platforms. This creates a recognizable and unified brand identity regardless of where customers encounter your business.

Integrated Customer Journey: Map out your customer journey and identify touchpoints across different platforms. Ensure a seamless transition between platforms, allowing customers to engage and make purchases effortlessly.

Cross-Platform Customer Support: Provide consistent customer support across all platforms. Utilize tools like chatbots, live chat, or helpdesk software to centralize customer inquiries and ensure a smooth support experience.

Data Integration: Integrate data from different platforms to gain a holistic view of your customers. Use customer data to personalize marketing efforts, tailor offers, and deliver relevant content based on their interactions across various channels.

Multichannel Selling: Explore e-commerce integrations that allow you to sell your products or services across multiple platforms. This can include integrating your Facebook Shop with an online store on platforms like Shopify or WooCommerce.

Remember to regularly analyze and optimize your omnichannel efforts based on customer feedback and data insights. Continuously monitor the performance of each platform, adapt your strategies, and experiment with new approaches to maximize your revenue potential.

By leveraging Facebook's integration options with other platforms, exploring cross-platform marketing and advertising strategies, and building an omnichannel presence, you can expand your reach, engage with a broader audience, and increase your revenue opportunities beyond Facebook alone.

Chapter 9. Future Trends and Opportunities on Facebook

A. Overview of emerging trends on the platform

B. Predictions for the future of monetization on Facebook

C. Strategies for staying ahead of the curve and adapting to changes

A. Overview of Emerging Trends on the Platform

Facebook is a dynamic platform that continually evolves with emerging trends. Here are some notable trends to keep an eye on:

Video Content Dominance: Video content continues to gain popularity on Facebook. Live videos, short-form videos, and video stories are driving higher engagement rates. Businesses should consider incorporating video content into their marketing strategies to capture audience attention.

Augmented Reality (AR): Facebook's AR capabilities, such as filters and effects, are becoming increasingly popular. AR can enhance user experiences, allowing businesses to showcase products, provide virtual try-on experiences, or create interactive branded content.

Messaging and Chatbots: Facebook Messenger and chatbot integration are growing trends. Businesses are leveraging Messenger to provide personalized customer support, send automated messages, and facilitate transactions. Chatbots can handle frequently asked questions and provide instant responses, enhancing customer satisfaction and engagement.

E-commerce Integration: Facebook's focus on e-commerce is evident through features like Facebook Shops and Marketplace. The platform is continuously enhancing its e-commerce capabilities, offering businesses opportunities to sell products directly on Facebook and reach a wider audience.

B. Predictions for the Future of Monetization on Facebook

Expanded Advertising Opportunities: Facebook will likely introduce new advertising formats and targeting options. This could include innovative ad placements, interactive ad experiences, or improved audience targeting capabilities. Advertisers can expect more opportunities to reach their target audience with tailored and engaging content.

Enhanced E-commerce Monetization: Facebook will likely continue to improve its e-commerce features and monetization options. Businesses can anticipate new ways to monetize their products or services, such as advanced product tagging, in-app purchases, or integrated payment systems.

Subscription-Based Content: Facebook may introduce subscription-based models for exclusive content or access to premium features. This can provide additional revenue streams for content creators and businesses while offering unique experiences to subscribers.

Influencer Marketing Evolution: Influencer marketing will continue to play a significant role on Facebook. Businesses may witness new collaborations and partnerships between influencers and brands. Facebook could introduce features to facilitate influencer marketing, such as dedicated influencer discovery tools or streamlined collaboration platforms.

C. Strategies for Staying Ahead of the Curve and Adapting to Changes

To stay ahead and adapt to changes on Facebook, consider the following strategies:

Regularly Monitor Platform Updates: Stay informed about Facebook's updates, new features, and policy changes. This allows you to proactively adjust your marketing strategies and take advantage of emerging opportunities.

Embrace New Formats and Features: Be open to experimenting with new formats, such as video content, AR effects, or interactive features. Stay creative and adapt your content strategies to leverage emerging trends that resonate with your target audience.

Stay Engaged with the Community: Actively engage with your audience, listen to their feedback, and address their needs. Encourage dialogue, respond to comments and messages promptly, and show authenticity and transparency in your interactions.

Test and Optimize: Continuously test different strategies, ad formats, targeting options, and content variations. Regularly analyze the results and optimize your campaigns based on data-driven insights.

Diversify Your Presence: While Facebook is essential, don't solely rely on it. Diversify your online presence by exploring other platforms and channels that align with your target audience. This ensures that you're not overly dependent on a single platform and allows you to reach a broader audience.

Embrace Data-Driven Decision Making: Leverage data analytics, audience insights, and performance metrics to make informed decisions. Regularly analyze your results, identify trends, and adjust your strategies accordingly.

By staying informed, embracing new features and formats, engaging with your audience, and leveraging data-driven insights, you can position your business to adapt and thrive in the ever-evolving landscape of Facebook. Continually evaluate your strategies, experiment with emerging trends, and be agile in your approach to seize future opportunities.

Conclusion

A. Recap of key concepts and strategies discussed

B. Final words of encouragement and inspiration

C. Call to action to start implementing the strategies and making money on Facebook

A. Recap of Key Concepts and Strategies Discussed

In this guide, we explored various concepts and strategies to help you succeed and make money on Facebook. Let's recap the key points:

Establishing a Strong Foundation:

Create a compelling Facebook business page.

Define your target audience and develop a clear brand identity.

Craft engaging and relevant content that resonates with your audience.

Effective Facebook Advertising:

Understand Facebook's advertising options and objectives.

Implement targeted ad campaigns to reach your desired audience.

Continuously monitor and optimize your ads based on key metrics.

Engaging and Growing Your Audience:

Foster meaningful interactions with your audience through authentic engagement.

Utilize Facebook Groups and events to build a community around your brand.

Leverage user-generated content and influencer partnerships for increased reach.

Maximizing Sales and Revenue:

Utilize Facebook's e-commerce features, such as Facebook Shops.

Implement effective sales funnels and conversion optimization strategies.

Leverage remarketing and personalized offers to drive sales.

Analyzing and Optimizing Results:

Track and analyze key metrics to measure campaign success.

Identify areas for improvement and optimize your strategies.

Conduct A/B testing and experiment with different approaches.

Beyond Facebook:

Leverage Facebook's integration options with other platforms.

Explore cross-platform marketing and advertising strategies.

Build an omnichannel presence to maximize revenue potential.

B. Final Words of Encouragement and Inspiration

Harnessing the power of Facebook for your business requires time, effort, and continuous adaptation. Remember that success doesn't typically happen overnight. Stay committed to your goals and remain passionate about providing value to your audience.

Embrace the challenges and setbacks as learning opportunities, and don't be afraid to try new strategies and experiment with innovative approaches. Stay open to change, stay ahead of emerging trends, and always prioritize the needs of your audience.

C. Call to Action to Start Implementing the Strategies and Making Money on Facebook

Now is the time to take action and start implementing the strategies discussed in this guide. Set specific goals, create a roadmap, and begin executing your Facebook marketing plan. Monitor your progress, analyze the results, and adapt your strategies based on data-driven insights.

Remember, success on Facebook is within your reach if you remain dedicated, innovative, and adaptable. So, take the first step, embrace the opportunities, and start making money on Facebook today!

Wishing you great success on your Facebook marketing journey!